CONTENTS

Any words appearing in the text in bold, **like this**, are explained in the Glossary.

INTRODUCTION

The modern Olympic Games began in 1896. With breaks during World Wars One and Two, they have been held at four-year intervals ever since. The first Games were staged in Greece, the home of the Olympics in ancient times. They returned to Athens for the spectacular 2004 Olympics.

One hundred years after the modern Olympics began, the 1996 organisers called their Games in Atlanta, USA, 'the largest peacetime social event in human history'. It would be hard to argue with that, even though they have continued to grow since then. The Games have become a wonderful celebration, not just of international sport, but also of healthy competition.

▲ Adolf Hitler (left) watches over the opening of the 1936 Olympic Games in Berlin, Germany.

TARNISH ON THE GOLD

Over the years, however, these peaceful Games have featured a high number of incidents, controversies, scandals, and even tragedies. In this book you can read about some of them. They range from the appalling organisation of the 1900 Games in Paris, to the outrage caused at Seoul in 1988 when 'the Fastest Man on Earth' tested positive for drugs after winning the 100 metres gold medal.

As you will see, many problems have arisen when Olympic sport has become mixed up with politics. Some people say that sport and politics are completely separate and should always stay that way. But as the Games grew bigger, and more and more people took an interest in them through the **media**, governments realised that they could use the Olympics to score political points over their rivals and enemies. Such a large international event will always have its tensions, and the 21st century continues to have its Olympic 'crises'.

THE OLYMPICS

CRISES AT THE OLYMPICS

REVISED AND UPDATED

Haydn Middleton

www.heinemann.co.uk/library
Visit our website to find out more information about Heinemann Library books.

To order:
☎ Phone 44 (0) 1865 888066
📠 Send a fax to 44 (0)1865 314091
💻 Visit the Heinemann Library Bookshop at www.heinemann.co.uk/library to browse our catalogue and order online.

First published in Great Britain by Heinemann Library, Halley Court, Jordan Hill, Oxford OX2 8EJ, part of Harcourt Education.
Heinemann Library is a registered trademark of Harcourt Education Ltd.

Editorial: Joanna Talbot
Design: Philippa Jenkins
Picture Research: Tracy Cummins
Production: Alison Parsons

Originated by Modern Age
Printed and bound in China by Leo Paper Group

ISBN 978 0 431 19161 4
12 11 10 09 08
10 9 8 7 6 5 4 3 2 1

British Library Cataloguing in Publication Data
Middleton, Haydn
    Crises at the olympics. – (The olympics)
    1.Olympic games (Ancient) – Juvenile literature
    2.Olympics Political aspects – Juvenile literature
    I.Title
    796.4·8

A full catalogue record for this book is available from the British Library.

Acknowledgements
The publishers would like to thank the following for permission to reproduce photographs:
Allsport pp. **6**, **8**, **10**, **12**, **13**, **15**, **19**, **24**, **25**; AP Photo pp. **26** (Julie Jacobson), **27** (Petros Giannakouris), **28** (Greg Bake, Filer); Corbis pp. **9** (Reuters/Yannis Behrakis), **14** (Bettmann), **29** Reuters/London 2012/Handout   IOC Olympic Museum p. **4**; Pressens Bild p. **5**; Associated Sports Photography pp. **17**, **20**; Colorsport pp. **16**, **18**, **21**; Popperfoto: p. **22**; Sporting Pictures (UK) Ltd p. **23**.

Cover photograph reproduced with permission of AP Photo/Amy Sancetta.

The publishers would like to thank John Townsend for his assistance with the preparation of this book.

No one knew this better than Adolf Hitler, whose Nazi Party ruled Germany when the Games were held in its capital city, Berlin, in 1936. Hitler planned to turn the Olympics into a **showcase** for the all-round superiority that he believed the German people had. On pages 10 and 11 you can see what became of this early attempt to abuse the true 'Olympic spirit'.

Political rivalry at the Games became especially open and bitter from 1952 onwards. The USA and **USSR**, global superpowers, seemed to be conducting a kind of peacetime warfare through their athletes. Their rivalry grew until, in 1980, the USA refused to send a team to the Olympic Games in the USSR. Then, in 1984, the USSR stayed away from the Los Angeles Games in the USA. You can read about these unfortunate **boycotts** on pages 20 and 21.

PROBLEMS IN PERSPECTIVE

Perhaps we should not be surprised that there have been so many Olympic crises. Any event that brings together competitors from so many nations (over 200 in recent Games) is bound to have problems. The dream of Olympic glory drives men and women from all over the world to great heights of achievement. The same dream has also been behind most of the stories that follow.

You can find out what Olympic outrage this **terrorist** was involved in on pages 14 and 15. ▼

IS THIS THE OLYMPIC GAMES?

Nowadays when the Olympic Games are being held, TV, radio, the Internet and newspapers make sure that people all over the world know about what is happening. But the first three Games of the modern era – at Athens in 1896, at Paris in 1900, and at St Louis, USA, in 1904 – were not so well publicised. Plenty of people remained blissfully ignorant that these Games were being staged. In fact, even some *competitors* were unaware that they were involved in the Olympics. Good organisation was not a feature of the modern Games' early history!

FARCE IN FRANCE

Compared to what followed in 1900 and 1904, the 1896 Games in Athens were a miracle of efficiency. The quality of the sport was often low, but the large crowds had a wonderful time – and afterwards many Greeks thought that the four-yearly Games should always be held in their country. But Baron de Coubertin, the 'Father' of the modern Olympic Movement, had an *international* vision – and the second Games were scheduled to take place in Paris, capital city of France, his own home country, in 1900.

This turned out to be a bad idea. That year, a great fair called the Universal Exposition was also being held in Paris. The Games – strung out from May to October – turned out to be little more than a sideshow within it. Spectators were few and far between, facilities and officials were often of a poor standard, and very few people seemed to know quite what was going on. American Margaret Abbott won the women's golf 'because', she later explained, 'all the French girls apparently misunderstood the nature of the game scheduled for that day and turned up to play in high heels and tight skirts'.

A poster for the 1900 Games in Paris, which were part of a much larger fair. Facilities for the athletes were very poor and there was little public interest in the Games. ▼

When these Games limped to an end, even de Coubertin had to admit: 'We have made a hash of our work.' He could only hope that the next Olympics – to be held across the Atlantic Ocean in St Louis in 1904 – would be a big improvement. But maybe he guessed they would not be, because he did not even travel all the way there himself – nor did many foreign competitors.

ABSURDITY IN AMERICA

The 1904 Games were held as part of the World's Fair. Again events were spread out over a period of months rather than days, and again the level of official incompetence was very high. One eyewitness said: 'I was not only present at a sporting contest but also at a fair where there were sports, where there was cheating, where monsters were exhibited as a joke.'

Maybe the lowest point came during the 'Anthropology Days', when athletic contests ranging from pole-climbing to stone-throwing were arranged purely for 'savage peoples' including Africans, Patagonians, and Sioux Indian tribesmen. Afterwards, one of the organisers concluded that 'the savage has been a very overrated man, from an athletic point of view'. Such an insulting and racist attitude to fellow human beings would not, of course, be tolerated today.

The 1904 Games in St Louis, USA, were the last to be linked to an international fair.

For a while after 1904, public interest was so low that it seemed there would be no more Games at all. Then in 1906 an **Interim** Games was held in Athens, in an attempt to get back to the spirit and success of 1896. In this, they very largely succeeded – thus whetting the world's appetite for the next official Games, in London in 1908. But London would have its own troubles…

DO YOU NEED ASSISTANCE?

The London Games of 1908 had their share of arguments about rules. Since then, the international federation governing each sport has controlled and judged individual competitions. But in 1908, countries had all kinds of rows, particularly over the marathon.

MARATHON MAYHEM

On a hot day in July, the marathon runners set off from Windsor Castle. They would run all the way to the Olympic stadium, just over 42 kilometres (26 miles) away at Shepherd's Bush. The last 352 metres (385 yards) were to be run around the stadium track, with the finishing line right in front of the **royal box**.

After about 32 kilometres (20 miles), South African Charles Hefferon was way out in front. However, a small Italian called Dorando Pietri was catching up fast. Hefferon began to tire about three kilometres (two miles) from the stadium, so someone in the crowd gave him a glass of champagne! He soon had stomach cramps and felt dizzy. Meanwhile, cheered on by the crowd, Pietri overtook him and entered the stadium first. But he ran the wrong way round the track and when officials rushed to tell him, Pietri collapsed. They got him back to his feet but he kept falling down every time they helped him up again.

Dorando Pietri is illegally helped over the finishing line at the 1908 marathon. When asked if the shortness of his legs was a problem for a marathon runner, he said that they were ideal since they were 'exactly long enough to reach from the hips to the ground'!

Suddenly another runner entered the stadium. It was John Hayes from the USA. As the crowd roared and Pietri fell again, Jack Andrews (the marathon's organiser) caught Pietri and carried him across the line!

The Italian flag was hoisted up the victory pole even as Hayes crossed the line himself. Naturally the Americans made a furious protest. It was upheld, and while Pietri was carried away on a stretcher, Hayes was declared the rightful winner. This avoided an all-out war between the US supporters and the British officials. The next day Pietri, fully recovered, claimed that he would have won without help. Queen Alexandra presented him with a **consolation** gold cup. Although he hadn't won a medal, the story of his run soon made him more famous than many true Olympic champions.

THE WRONG KIND OF HELP

In the men's marathon at Athens in 2004, after 36 kilometres (22 miles), Brazilian Vanderlei Lima's chance of winning was destroyed by a man from the crowd who pushed Lima off the road. The attacker was immediately tackled by another spectator and Lima broke free, returning to the race unhurt. Other runners soon overtook him but when he entered the stadium, Lima received a loud cheer from the crowd, who had seen the incident on giant-screen televisions. Lima still managed to win the bronze medal.

MORE MARATHON HEADLINES

In the 2004 Athens Olympics, Great Britain's Paula Radcliffe was the favourite to win the marathon. She had suffered a leg injury two weeks before the race and took a high dose of anti-inflammatory drugs. This affected her stomach's ability to absorb food. Her lack of energy, as well as the heat, led to her withdrawing from the race after 36 kilometres (22 miles).

Paula Radcliffe's troubles didn't end with the marathon. Still suffering from its effects, she later withdrew from the 10,000-metre race as well.

◄

RACING AGAINST RACISM

The International Olympic Committee (IOC) decides where each Olympic Games is to be held. It takes its decision several years in advance. Then the host city has plenty of time to make all the necessary preparations. In 1931 the IOC decided that the 1936 Games would be held in Berlin, the capital of Germany. The Germans were one of the world's leading sporting nations, and they could be relied on to organise a successful Olympics. But then, in 1933, something unforeseen happened. A new political party was elected to power in Germany. Its name was the National Socialist German Workers' Party – Nazi for short – and its leader was Adolf Hitler.

▲ The official poster for the 1936 Olympics.

OLYMPIC SPIRIT OR OLYMPIC SPITE?

Soon people inside and beyond Germany learned that Hitler and his followers held racist views. These included the belief that white-skinned, 'racially pure' Germans were superior in all ways to other peoples, particularly Jews or blacks. Signs with messages like 'Dogs and Jews are not allowed' appeared in Germany. The Nuremberg Laws of 1935 declared Jews to be 'subhuman'. It became clear that Hitler wanted to use the Berlin Games of August 1936 as a **showcase** for his idea of the German 'Super Race'.

Jewish communities outside Germany called for a **boycott** of the Games. In the USA there was an especially strong campaign. But the Nazis assured the IOC that they would abide by the rules of Olympic competition. Two 'half-Jews' were even selected for the German national team. So the Games went ahead as planned.

Jesse Owens in action. Four years after his death in 1980 a Berlin street was renamed after him – a fitting tribute to one of the greatest Olympians of all. ▶

TRIUMPH OF THE 'BLACK MERCENARIES'

Before 1936 Germany had not excelled in **track and field** events. But early in the Berlin Games, policeman Hans Woellke became the first German track-and-field gold medallist ever – in the shot-put. Hitler and his supporters were delighted. But their joy was not going to last.

The USA ended up with 25 medals in track and field – and thirteen were won by African-Americans, whom the Nazis called 'black **mercenaries**'. One of these supreme black athletes was Jesse Owens, gold medallist in the 100 metres, 200 metres, long jump and 4 × 100-metre relay. In spite of all the Nazi **propaganda**, the German people made Owens the hero of the Games. They even thrust autograph books through his Olympic-village bedroom window while he was trying to get some sleep!

There is a story that after Owens won the 100 metres final, a furious Hitler refused to meet him – even though he had congratulated other gold medallists. This may or may not be true. What *is* true is that when Owens went home to the USA, American President Franklin D. Roosevelt failed to invite him to the White House. He did not even send him a letter of praise on his awesome Olympic feats. Thanks to racial laws in the USA, Owens, like other black people, was not seen as equal to his white fellow-Americans. His Olympic brilliance gave a huge boost to the pride of African-Americans. But even by the time of the 1968 Olympics, long after Hitler and his hateful ideas had disappeared, true racial equality had still not been achieved in the USA.

PODIUM PROTESTS

The 1968 Games in Mexico City were controversial even before they began. The Olympics had never been held at such **altitude** before – over 2,000 metres (6,562 feet) above sea level. Many experts feared that athletes unused to the very thin air might die from pushing themselves too hard. These were also the Games in which sex-tests were to be introduced. (This was because some women were suspected of chemically 'improving' their bodies with human growth hormones, thus making themselves – technically – men!)

And then, ten days before the Games were due to begin, Mexico City became the scene of a bloodbath when the Mexican army opened fire on a big student **demonstration**. About 260 people were killed and around 1,200 injured. Shock waves from this were felt all around the sporting world. But the International Olympic Committee called it an 'internal affair' which was 'under control'. The Games could still go on – under their official slogan: 'Everything is possible with peace.'

'AMERICAN' OR 'NEGRO'?
Once the Games began, the biggest debate came after the 200 metres final for men. Black American Tommie Smith cruised home in a new world-record time of 19.83 seconds. In third place was fellow-black-American John Carlos. Both men belonged to the Olympic Project for Human Rights – a group of athletes who campaigned for better treatment for blacks in the USA – and they wanted the world to know about racial **inequality** there.

Tommie Smith and John Carlos make their peaceful protest on the podium in Mexico City, 1968. When Carlos was accused of 'tainting' the Games by making a political point, he said the Olympics were already highly political. 'Why do they play national anthems?…' he asked. 'Why can't everyone wear the same colours but wear numbers to tell them apart? What happened to the Olympic ideal of man against man?'

So when they stepped up onto the podium to collect their medals, they took off their shoes. And when the American anthem played, they both bowed their heads and raised a black-gloved hand in a 'Black Power' salute.

They explained later that their bare feet were a reminder of black American poverty, and their clenched fists showed black strength and unity. 'White America will only give us credit for an Olympic victory,' said Carlos. 'They'll say I'm an American, but if I did something bad, they'd say I was a Negro.' In the eyes of the US Olympic Committee, this protest was something bad. Both men were quickly banned from the team and ordered out of the Olympic village. Back at home, they then found it hard to make a living for many years. But they had drawn the world's attention to a very big problem – and in a completely peaceful way.

FLASHBACK TO 1936

At the Berlin Games of 1936 the marathon was won in style by Korean athlete Sohn Kee-Chung. Fellow-Korean Nam Seung-Yong picked up the bronze. But at that time their homeland was being **occupied** by Japan. So they were forced to run in the colours of Japan, and they even had to take Japanese names. To show their dissatisfaction, after receiving their medals they bowed their heads in silent protest while the Japanese national anthem was played.

In later years Sohn was able to enjoy the Games a little more. At the opening ceremony in 1948 he carried the flag of a newly-freed South Korea. And in 1988 in Seoul, South Korea's capital, he carried the Olympic torch into the stadium, at the age of 76.

The USA's gold-medal-winning 4 × 400 m team leaves the arena in Mexico City with a clenched-fist salute, showing support for their fellow African-Americans. ▶

BLACK SEPTEMBER

The 1972 Games were held in Munich, West Germany. All was set to make these the best Games ever. To make sure that 27 African nations did not carry out their threat to **boycott** the Games, the International Olympic Committee (IOC) expelled Rhodesia (now called Zimbabwe) for its policy of **white supremacy**.

It now seemed that little could go wrong. In purely sporting terms, very little did. With over 4,000 representatives of the world's **media** present, records tumbled as never before. But the Games' sheer size, and the interest they created all over the world, also attracted to Munich people with *no* interest in sport. On the morning of 5 September they made their presence felt.

WORST-CASE SCENARIO

The Munich Games were meant to be really friendly. As a result, security was quite minimal. That was how eight Palestinian Arab **terrorists** managed to get into the Olympic Village. Ever since 1948, Arabs and Israelis had been at odds with each other in the Middle East. On 5 September 1972 the Arabs headed for the Israeli quarters, killed two people there and took nine more as **hostages**.

On 6 September 1972, 80,000 people filled the Olympic stadium in Munich to remember those who had died in the Olympic Games' worst act of terrorism. ▶

They then demanded the release of 200 Arab prisoners from Israeli jails – as well as a safe passage to Egypt for themselves. After long negotiations, the terrorists and their hostages were allowed to go to the military airport. There, West German marksmen killed three of the terrorists. But a gun battle followed, in which all nine Israeli hostages were killed, along with two more Arabs and a policeman. After such an awful tragedy what could happen next?

THE GAMES MUST GO ON

Some people felt that the Games should now be declared over, and a few athletes did leave Munich for fear of another terrorist attack. But finally the IOC decided to continue the programme.

The aim of the terrorists had been to disrupt the Games, argued IOC President Avery Brundage, so why should they get what they wanted? Besides, if they managed to stop the Olympics in its tracks, how many other similar groups might try to do the same in future? The Israeli officials were in full agreement with this. The Games went on with their blessing. And since that dreadful day in 1972, terrorism has not been a major Olympic issue – but providing tight security *has* been.

▲ After the tragedy, the 1972 Games continued – but lesser controversies continued to occur. Despite his lunge for the line in the 800 m final, Russian Yevgeny Arzhanov lost to American Dave Wottle (in the cap) by 0.03 seconds. Wottle was so shocked at winning that he forgot to take off his cap during the national anthem – people thought he was making a protest of some kind.

ATLANTA TERROR

The 1996 Games in Atlanta, USA, saw another act of violence. A terrorist acting alone set off a bomb in the Centennial Olympic Park, killing two spectators and wounding more than 100 others. But within days the Park reopened and the fans flocked back. Just as in Munich 24 years before, the show had to go on, in spite of the cowardly attempt to disrupt it.

MISERY IN MONTREAL

Sporting achievements took most of the headlines at the 1976 Games in Montreal, Canada, but in financial terms they could hardly have been more disastrous. For a variety of reasons, the cost of staging the Olympics in 1976 was much higher than the cost of staging them in Munich four years earlier. When the Games finished, the taxpayers of Montreal had to pay off an unpaid amount of US$1 billion. It took them until 1996 – just before the Atlanta Games – to do this. Yet Mayor Jean Drapeau had claimed 'the Games could no more produce a deficit than a man could have a baby'!

BOYCOTTS AND BANS

Once the Games got under way, there were around 1,000 fewer competitors than in Munich. This was because more than 30 countries were either banned or refused to take part. As in 1971, Rhodesia (now Zimbabwe) was banned because blacks and whites were still kept separate due to that country's system of **white supremacy**. The island of Taiwan withdrew because the Canadian Government refused to recognise it as the Republic of China – a title that it disputed with mainland, **Communist**, China. But by far the largest number of absentee (missing) nations came from Africa. Their reason for staying away was tied up with rugby union – not even an Olympic sport.

When the 1976 Games opened in Montreal, work on the Olympic facilities was still going on. This was due partly to bad weather conditions during the long winter, partly to workers' strikes, and partly to a serious lack of funds. This lack of funds was not helped by the constructors of the Olympic stadium hiring 33 cranes at a cost of $1 million – and then never even using some of them! It would have been cheaper to have bought the cranes outright. A much tighter security operation, after the terrorist outrage at the Munich Games, also contributed to the vast expense. ▼

The official poster for the 1976 Games in Montreal, which have gone down in Olympic history as a financial disaster. ▶

CANADA
1976

The awesome New Zealand rugby team is called the All Blacks (after the colour of their kit). The All Blacks had recently made a tour of South Africa which, like Rhodesia, was banned from the Olympics on account of its **apartheid** policy. Over 20 African nations, plus Guyana and Iraq, now demanded that the International Olympic Committee (IOC) should ban New Zealand from the 1976 Olympics. When the IOC refused, the protesting nations, led by Tanzania, took their own action by **boycotting** the Games – which were all the poorer for their absence.

BURNING OF THE BOAT

In spite of all these troubles, the Montreal Olympics were still hugely enjoyable to watch and take part in. Triple-gold medallist Nadia Comaneci, a fourteen-year-old Romanian gymnast, became a popular symbol of all that was right about the Games. Even so, not everyone was happy. Two British yachtsmen Allen Warren and David Hunt, finished fourteenth out of sixteen entries in the Tempest class. After the final race, they calmly set their boat on fire, then waded ashore to watch it burn! 'I tried to persuade my skipper [Warren] to burn with the ship,' joked Hunt, 'but he wouldn't agree.'

The last disappointment came for the poor Canadians themselves. The final medal table showed not a single gold for the host country – the first time that had ever happened at the Summer Games!

MEDAL MUDDLE

The Olympic Charter clearly states that 'the Olympic Games are competitions between athletes ... and not between countries'. It has not always seemed that way. Until 1908 athletes entered the Games as individuals, not as chosen members of a national team. That was the original Olympic ideal. Since then, however, one of the most popular features of any Games has been the medals table.

The International Olympic Committee still does not officially recognise national medal totals. But for the **media** and the public, they are often too fascinating to ignore. After all, how else can you tell at a glance which country is 'winning' the Games?

Valeri Borzov of the USSR wins the 200 m gold at the 1972 Games. He refused to give an interview after the race because, he said, American journalists had insulted him after he won the 100 m final.

WHO ARE THE CHAMPIONS?

The two tables show the final medals totals at the 1928 Games in Amsterdam and then at the 1976 Games in Montreal. In 1928 all the leading nations came from Europe and North America. By 1976 that had changed, with Cuba, Japan, and the part-Asiatic **USSR** making appearances.

In that year, all top ten nations were under **Communist** rule except for the USA, West Germany, and Japan. Throughout the **Cold War** period, many Communist governments sponsored sport very heavily – and reaped the reward in Olympic gold medals.

NATIONAL MEDAL TOTALS, 1928 AND 1976							
Amsterdam 1928				Montreal 1976			
	G	S	B		G	S	B
USA	22	18	16	USSR	49	41	35
Germany	10	7	14	East Germany	40	25	25
Finland	8	8	9	USA	34	35	25
Sweden	7	6	12	West Germany	10	12	17
Italy	7	5	7	Japan	9	6	10
Switzerland	7	4	4	Poland	7	6	13
France	6	10	5	Bulgaria	6	9	7
Netherlands	6	9	4	Cuba	6	4	3
Hungary	4	5	0	Romania	4	9	14
Canada	4	4	7	Hungary	4	5	13
G = gold; **S** = silver; **B** = bronze							
A nation's position in the medals table is determined by its gold-medal count. If a nation has no gold medals, it is ranked according to its silver or its bronze count.							

The USA had never lost a basketball match at the Olympics before 1972. In 1988, they had to settle for the bronze medal as two Communist nations, the USSR and Yugoslavia, played each other in the final. ▶

According to one East German official at Montreal in 1976, this 'proved the success of our socialist (Communist) system and our training methods'. In Western countries, such as the USA and West Germany, governments did not usually get so directly involved, but were just as keen to see their athletes do well. In a way, the struggle to win gold became a kind of sporting warfare.

BASKETBALL BATTLE

Some athletes were dismayed by this international rivalry – especially between the USA and the USSR. Montreal champion swimmer John Naber said: 'Gold medals don't mean the White House is better than the **Kremlin**. It means I swam faster than anyone else, that's all.' But few could doubt that more than mere sport was at stake n Munich in 1972, when the USA took on the USSR in the Games' final basketball match.

Ever since 1936, when the sport first figured at the Games, the USA had never lost a game. And when the horn sounded for the end of this one, they were ahead by 50 points to 49. But the Brazilian referee overruled the clock. The game was briefly restarted, then the horn sounded again. Now a higher official ruled that, thanks to an earlier mix-up, three more seconds should be added on. The USSR team pulled off a court-long move which ended with a basket. And amid enormous uproar, they were given the victory by 51 points to 50. The US team, disgusted at having been 'cheated', refused to accept their silver medals. To lose any Olympic match was bad enough. But to lose to the USSR – and in such controversial circumstances – *that* was almost unbearable.

POLITICS STOPPED PLAY

'In ancient days,' one-time International Olympic Committee (IOC) President Avery Brundage once said, 'nations stopped wars to compete in the Games. Nowadays we stop the Olympics to continue our wars.' Political conflict certainly had an impact on the Games in 1980.

US President Jimmy Carter was the man behind the boycott of the 1980 Games in Moscow. ▼

THE NEARLY MAN

David Wallechinsky described in his brilliant *Complete Book of the Olympics* how the various boycotts of the 1970s and 1980s affected one unlucky individual. Bruce Kennedy was an excellent javelin-thrower from Rhodesia. In 1972, he was selected for the Rhodesian team to travel to Munich. But the IOC banned Rhodesia from taking part because of the racist system of government in that country.

He was selected again for Montreal in 1976, but Rhodesia was still excluded. Then, by marrying an American citizen, he qualified for the USA team which would go to Moscow in 1980. That team, of course, never arrived in the USSR thanks to the boycott over the USSR's invasion of Afghanistan. By then, though, Rhodesia (renamed Zimbabwe) had been allowed back into the Olympic Games.

In 1984 Kennedy was absolutely determined to get into an Olympic stadium. And at last he managed it – as an usher!

In 1980 Alan Wells (left) became only the second Briton to win the 100 m at the Olympic Games. American athletes, who were absent from Moscow, had won twelve of the previous eighteen contests.

NO GO FOR MOSCOW

Political rivalry between the USA and the **USSR** had figured in most Games since 1952. It came to a head at the 1980 Olympics – and threatened to wreck the Olympic Movement altogether. These Games were due to be held in Moscow, the capital city of the **Communist**-ruled USSR (otherwise known as the Soviet Union). In 1979, Soviet forces had invaded Afghanistan – and US President Jimmy Carter responded with a call to **boycott** the 1980 Games. As a result, an almighty controversy broke out.

A Dutch member of the IOC said it was 'unjust to make athletes the conscience of the world'. Each National Olympic Committee had to decide what to do. Rule 28 of the Olympic Charter says that the Committees 'must be **autonomous** and must resist all pressure of any kind whatsoever, whether of a political, religious or economic nature'. Some governments friendly to the USA, such as Britain and Australia, backed the boycott but said their athletes could choose for themselves whether to travel to Moscow. That was not quite so easy for American athletes – President Carter threatened to **revoke** the passport of any competitor who tried to get to the USSR.

In the end only 80 nations took part in the Moscow Games (in 1984 there would be 140). But more world records were set than in 1976, and there were plenty of supremely memorable contests. But many fans believed the Games were 'devalued' by the absence of the USA, West Germany, China, Japan, and many other great sporting nations in the biggest Olympic boycott yet.

THE RUSSIANS AREN'T COMING — BUT ZOLA BUDD IS!

After the American-led **boycott** of the 1980 Games in the **USSR**, it was the USA's turn to stage the 1984 Games. And guess what? The USSR organised its own fourteen-nation boycott! The Soviet authorities refused to let their athletes attend partly as a protest over **commercialisation** (see picture below) and partly due to doubts about the level of security in Los Angeles. It seemed clear to many, however, that this was a simple act of revenge for the 1980 boycott.

COLLISION COURSE

A new event was due to appear in the **track-and-field** programme at Los Angeles: the 3,000 metres for women. Two runners with very different backgrounds were determined to take part in it: Mary Decker of the USA and South African Zola Budd. Decker had been an infant **prodigy**. At the age of twelve, she ran a marathon in just over three hours, a 440 metres, an 880 metres, a mile race then a two-mile race — all in the space of one week! But around the age of fifteen all the running badly affected her growing body, and she missed the 1976 Games through illness. By 1980, however, she was back with a vengeance: setting a world record for the mile, and raring to take on the world's best in the Moscow Games of 1980. The boycott shattered that dream, but it only made her more determined to run in Los Angeles — her home town — in 1984.

British **decathlon** gold-medallist Daley Thompson models an interesting T-shirt in Los Angeles. The back of the shirt criticised the broadcasts of the ABC television network, which focused closely on American winners at the expense of other nations.

ABC had paid US$225 million for exclusive TV transmission rights — a massive step up from the US$394,000 fee paid by the CBS TV network in 1960. In the eyes of some, this led to an unacceptable commercialisation of the Games. ▼

Zola Budd's home town was Bloemfontein, South Africa. She had a poster of her heroine, Decker, on her bedroom wall. But by 1983, aged seventeen and running barefoot, she was ranked number one in the world at 5,000 metres. And in January 1984, she broke Decker's world record at that distance by seven seconds. But to get to Los Angeles, Budd had to change her nationality. As a South African, she was barred from competing (see page 19). So she moved to Britain, her grandfather's homeland, became a British citizen instead, and got into the British team.

DECKER ON THE DECK

Thus the stage was set for a great Decker–Budd showdown in Los Angeles. It turned out to be one of the most controversial races ever. After 1,700 metres Budd led, followed closely by Decker. What happened next depended on whose side you took. Budd and Decker got into a tangle, and Budd was briefly thrown off balance. Five strides later, it happened again. Decker tripped over Budd's leg, cutting the barefoot leader's heel with her spikes. Decker fell awkwardly and was out of the race in agony.

Budd ran on – bleeding from the clash, and soon crying too because Decker's home crowd of over 85,000 was booing her so loudly. She came in seventh, and was then disqualified for 'causing' Decker's downfall. Later, that decision was overruled, but a huge dispute blew up between the American and British **media** over who had been at fault. In the end, almost everyone agreed that it had been an unfortunate accident. But neither woman was destined to win any medal at all at future Games.

Budd (151) vs Decker (373). Many events in 1984 were scheduled at American TV's main viewing time, even though this was the middle of the night in Europe.

FAILING THE TEST

For many people, the men's 100-metre sprint is *the* big Olympic event. As the athletes lined up for the 100 metres final at Seoul in 1988, the world held its breath. In under ten seconds, the World's Fastest Man would be revealed. Carl Lewis, the 1984 champion, was running. So was world-record holder Ben Johnson from Canada. They had not always got on well. Lewis suspected that Johnson took illegal drugs called steroids to 'improve' his performance. Just 9.79 seconds later, Johnson triumphantly thrust his arm in the air as he smashed his own world record. Second-placed Lewis was surer than ever that Johnson had cheated. And at the post-race drug test, he was proved right.

'I KNOW WHAT IT'S LIKE TO CHEAT'

Drug-testing of urine samples was introduced at the 1968 Olympics. Since then 42 athletes had been disqualified – and disgraced – for failing their tests. Ben Johnson was the 43rd but no star so famous had been caught before.

PASSING THE TEST!

At the 1968 Games in Mexico, British bricklayer Chris Finnegan won the middleweight boxing crown. He could barely describe his feelings: 'the nearest I've felt to it was when walking down the aisle with my old woman after our wedding ... only there was no gold medal at the end of that!' But then he had to perform again – by giving a urine sample that could be tested for drugs. To everyone's frustration, it took him until 1.40 the next morning before he could provide the sample – then pass the test.

Ben Johnson of Canada won the Seoul 100 m final in 1988 by a margin that was just too big to be true.

Shock waves from Seoul rippled all over the world. And it got worse. Later enquiries showed that Johnson had been taking steroids since 1981 – plus growth hormones which were taken from human corpses! In 1989 Johnson publicly confessed and pleaded with young athletes not to follow his example. 'It happened to me,' he said in tears. 'I've been there. I know what it's like to cheat.'

ALL IN THE BLOOD

Finland's Lasse Viren won the 5,000 m and 10,000 m at both the 1972 and 1976 Games. Although no one could prove it, some suspected him of blood doping to achieve his great Olympic feats. This technique, which was not then illegal, involved taking out some of an athlete's blood, storing it for a week or two, then re-injecting it just before a big race. This would improve the body's intake of oxygen.

Viren always laughed at the suspicions, and said he trained on reindeer milk. But in 1984, fellow Finn Martti Vainio lost his 10,000 m silver medal when traces of a steroid were found in his sample. It is believed that he stopped *taking* steroids three weeks before the race – hoping not to be caught – but thanks to blood doping, steroids were brought back into his bloodstream.

◄ Super-sprinter Florence Griffith Joyner of the USA won three gold medals at Seoul. Some people suspected Flojo of using drugs to achieve phenomenal times after an unspectacular start to her career. She passed every drug test she took, but retired in 1989 just before random (unannounced) testing came in.

Sadly she died of a heart seizure in 1998, aged only 38. People who still suspected her pointed out that steroid use can lead, in the long term, to an overloading of the heart and damage to the **arteries**. One of the sad effects of drugtaking in sport is that *any* amazing feat immediately seems suspicious, even if the sportsman or woman is completely innocent.

CHASING THE CHEATS

The Olympics of the 21st century continue the fight to rid the Games of cheating. As more sophisticated drugs become available for athletes to use, more and better tests will expose those who deliberately cheat.

The Athens Games of 2004 were worse than any other for drug offences, but the International Olympic Committee (IOC) took the cheats head-on. Not since Ben Johnson in Seoul had a track-and-field gold medallist been stripped of a gold medal. Now there were three. Russian shot-put champion Irina Korzhanenko tested positive for steroids. Hungarian discus thrower Robert Fazekas and another Hungarian, hammer thrower Adrian Annus, both lost their gold medals for refusing to give urine samples.

The IOC president, Jacques Rogge, said that the Athens Games had been successful by exposing the few cheats. More than 3,000 tests were carried out, a 25 percent increase on the number conducted in Sydney four years before. 'You have 10,500 athletes in the Olympic village. You do not have 10,500 saints,' Rogge said. 'You will always have cheats.'

Irina Korzhanenko of Russia was later stripped of her gold medal in the shot-put in the Athens Olympics after testing positive for the same steroid that Ben Johnson had used 16 years earlier. ►

GONE MISSING

The Athens Games began with something of a crisis for the Greek officials. Two of their own runners had to withdraw from the Games, and this threatened to cast a cloud over the entire Games even before they had begun. Ekaterini Thanou and Kostas Kenteris made headline news when they failed to turn up for a drugs test. They were Greece's biggest athletic stars and best medal hopes. They were accused of missing a drugs test and staging a motorcycle accident to avoid testers on the eve of the Games. The embarrassed sprinters withdrew from the Games rather than face likely expulsion by the IOC.

Greek sprinter Kostas Kenteris was suspended for two years after the 2004 Athens Olympics. He said he planned to make his comeback at the 2008 Beijing Olympics. ▼

DRUG TESTS FOR ALL?

The Beijing Olympics in 2008 will test 4,500 competitors for drugs. London's preparations for the Olympics in 2012 include plans to test half of all athletes for performance-enhancing drugs. The IOC president, Jacques Rogge, said, 'It is becoming more and more difficult to cheat at the Olympics.'

OLYMPIC DREAM OR OLYMPIC NIGHTMARE?

No Olympic Games will be without their troubles and tensions. Organising so many events, people, and facilities, all under the constant glare of world publicity, must be any planner's nightmare. And yet, every four years, many cities join the frantic race to realise their dream of hosting a future Olympics. As soon as the next venue is decided and the winning city is declared, newspapers are full of all the impending problems. The 21st century has seen its share of 'crises at the Olympics'.

Beijing is making a huge effort to clean up its polluted streets before the 2008 Games.

Italian president enters Olympics crisis

When the mayor of Turin said he was resigning because there was not enough money for the 2006 Turin Olympics organising committee to do its job properly, the Italian president at the time, Carlo Ciampi, stepped in. 'Cooperation is needed in the national interest,' he said. Eventually, the 2006 Winter Olympics went ahead without a crisis.

2004 Olympics hit by crisis

Iran's world judo champion Arash Miresmaeili refused to compete against an Israeli. This caused a fresh crisis at the Olympic Games, where race, creed or colour are not allowed to interfere with sport. In the end, he was disqualified for being over the correct weight for his sport.

Will pollution overshadow the 2008 Olympics?

The Beijing Organising Committee for the 2008 Games announced that there is a huge effort under way to bring Beijing's air pollution in line with global standards before the 2008 Olympic Games. The city plans to move more than 100 factories outside the city and replace 300,000 polluting vehicles with cleaner ones. It is also seeking to replace coal furnaces with natural gas furnaces before the Olympic Games to make the Beijing air cleaner.

2010 Games in crisis

The true cost of the 2010 Winter Olympic Games in Vancouver, Canada, is at least $2.5 billion. This figure could still soar higher and may even result in the delay of sporting facilities, and damage athletes' chances to win gold medals, some people fear.

2012 Olympics bill could hit £9 billion

The true cost of the 2012 Olympics could hit a staggering £9 billion, according to reports. The London Olympic organisers admitted that the new budget would be much higher than first thought because of extra security costs, regeneration projects, and tax bills.

WATER CRISIS IN ATHENS

The mayor of Athens said she wasn't sure if the city's water company would be able to meet peak demands for water during the 2004 Olympics in August. Luckily, there was still enough water to fill the swimming pool!

The new facilities being built for the London 2012 Olympics – including this aquatic centre – are a major expense for the city.

BUT THE SHOW GOES ON!

Despite all the uncertainties and doubts about every Olympic Games since they first began, one thing is sure: for however long they remain, the Olympic Games will always attract world attention, criticism, controversy, frustration, tension, and fears. There will also be the occasional crisis. But somehow, however scary the nightmares, the Olympic dream seems set to last.

GLOSSARY

altitude height above sea level

apartheid policy of keeping black people apart from, and saying they are inferior to, whites

artery part of the human body which helps to convey blood from the heart

autonomous self-governing, free from outside interference

boycott to refuse to have anything to do with a person, country or event

Cold War period, after World War Two, of unfriendly relations between the USA and the USSR, which never became real warfare

commercialisation attempt to make money from something

Communism political, economic, and social system that has state-owned land, factories, and means of production. After World War Two, the USSR introduced communism into much of eastern Europe.

consolation a prize given not for winning, but for just missing out

decathlon competition containing ten different events: 100 metres, 110 metres hurdles, 400 metres, 1500 metres, high jump, long jump, pole vault, javelin, discus, and shot-put

demonstration public protest about an issue

hostage someone who is held as a prisoner until certain demands are met

inequality lack of fairness between different groups in society

interim taking place in between official Games

Kremlin headquarters of the government of the USSR

media plural of medium (of communication), for example newspapers, magazines, TV, and radio

mercenary person who is purely working for pay or other rewards

occupied invaded and held by force

pentathlon competition containing five different events

prodigy someone, especially a child, who is very talented

propaganda information put out to convince people of an idea or a view

revoke take away

royal box special seats from which a royal family views public events

showcase acting as an advertisement for something

terrorist someone who uses violence to force a government to do what he or she wants

track and field sporting events which involve running, jumping, throwing and walking – such as the 100 metres or the javelin

USSR a Communist country, including Russia and many smaller nations, which broke up in 1991

white supremacy political arrangement or system of government by which white people, although small in numbers, have more rights and privileges than the black majority

FIND OUT MORE

USING THE INTERNET

Explore the Internet to find out more about the past crises at the Olympics or to see pictures of the most recent Games. You can use a search engine such as www.yahooligans.com, or ask a question at www.ask.com. To find out more about crises at the Olympics, you could search by typing in key words such as Olympic crisis, Munich Olympics, or Olympics+drugs.

These are some useful websites to look at to find more information:

http://www.infoplease.com/spot/olympicstimeline.html
This website provides an Olympics timeline.

http://www.olympic.org
This is the official website of the Olympic Movement, with all the latest news and a countdown to the next Games.

http://www.paralympic.org
This is the official website of the IPC (International Paralympic Committee).

http://www.enchantedlearning.com/olympics/
This website provides general information and activities.

BOOKS

The Olympics: Athens to Athens 1896-2004, M. Jacques Rogge (Weidenfeld Nicolson Illustrated, 2004)

The Olympics: Facts, Figures and Fun, Liam McCann (Artists' and Photographers' Press Ltd, 2006)

Total Olympics: The Complete Record and History of the Olympic Games, Bill Mallon (Total Sports, 2001)

INDEX